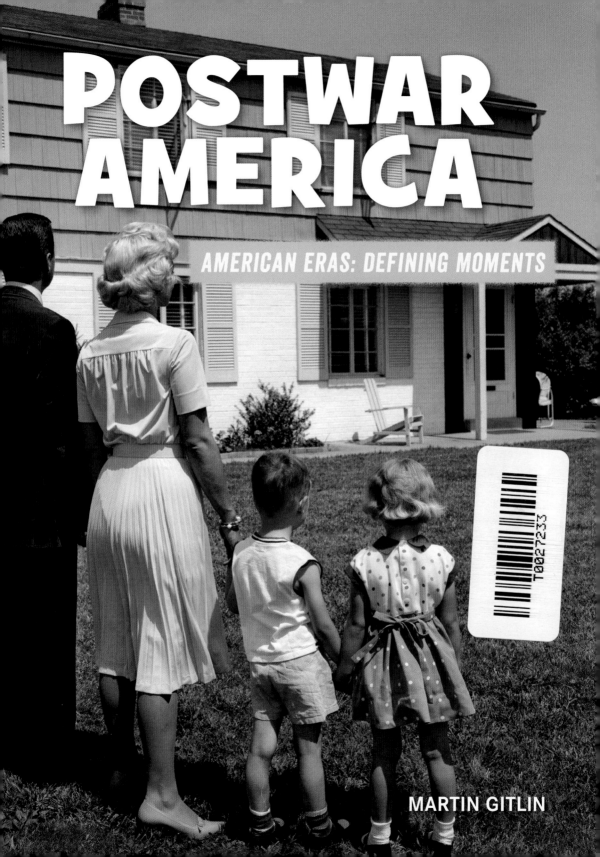

POSTWAR AMERICA

AMERICAN ERAS: DEFINING MOMENTS

MARTIN GITLIN

CHERRY LAKE PRESS

Published in the United States of America by Cherry Lake Publishing Group
Ann Arbor, Michigan
www.cherrylakepublishing.com

Content Adviser: Kevin Whinnery, MA, History
Reading Adviser: Beth Walker Gambro, MS, Ed., Reading Consultant, Yorkville, IL
Photo Credits: © ClassicStock/Alamy Stock Photo, cover, 1; © Everett Collection/Shutterstock, 5;
    © National Archives Catalog/NA Identifier: 531340, 7; © Photo by United States. Army Air Forces/
    Library of Congress/LOC Control No. 2002722137, 8; © National Archives Catalog/NA Identifier
    16685049, 9; © Everett Collection/Shutterstock, 10; © National Archives Catalog/NA Identifier
    6003286, 11; © Photo by Warren K. Leffler/Library of Congress/LOC Control No. 2017658325, 12;
    © National Archives Catalog/Photo title "Youth March for Integrated Schools", 15; © Library of
    Congress/LOC Control No. 2015648524, 16; © The Visibility Project, Claudette Colvin/Wikimedia, 17;
    © National Archives Catalog/NA Identifier 7718884, 18; © atlantic-kid/istock, 21; © National
    Archives Catalog/NA Identifier 6361898, 22; © Photo by Harris & Ewing/Library of Congress/LOC
    Control No. 2016883677, 23; © Everett Collection/Shutterstock, 24; © Photo by Marion S. Trikosko/
    Library of Congress/LOC Control No. 2017657598, 25; © Digital museum/picryl, 26; ©jmanaugh3/
    Shutterstock, 28

Copyright © 2022 by Cherry Lake Publishing Group
All rights reserved. No part of this book may be reproduced or utilized in any form or by any means
without written permission from the publisher.

Cherry Lake Press is an imprint of Cherry Lake Publishing Group.

Library of Congress Cataloging-in-Publication Data
Names: Gitlin, Marty, author.
Title: Postwar America / by Martin Gitlin.
Description: Ann Arbor, Michigan : Cherry Lake Publishing Group, [2022] | Series: American eras:
    defining moments | Includes bibliographical references and index.
Identifiers: LCCN 2021007859 (print) | LCCN 2021007860 (ebook) | ISBN 9781534187399 (hardcover) |
    ISBN 9781534188792 (paperback) | ISBN 9781534190191 (pdf) | ISBN 9781534191594 (ebook)
Subjects: LCSH: United States—History—1945-1953—Juvenile literature. | United States—
    History—1953-1961—Juvenile literature. | Civil rights movements—United States—History—Juvenile
    literature. | Cold War—Juvenile literature.
Classification: LCC E813 .G55 2021 (print) | LCC E813 (ebook) | DDC 973.921—dc23
LC record available at https://lccn.loc.gov/2021007859
LC ebook record available at https://lccn.loc.gov/2021007860

Cherry Lake Publishing Group would like to acknowledge the work of the Partnership for 21st Century
Learning, a Network of Battelle for Kids. Please visit http://www.battelleforkids.org/networks/p21
for more information.

Printed in the United States of America
Corporate Graphics

ABOUT THE AUTHOR

Martin Gitlin has written more than 150 educational books. He also won more than 45 awards
during his 11-year career as a newspaper journalist. Gitlin lives in Cleveland, Ohio.

TABLE OF CONTENTS

The guns had finally fallen silent. The last bomb had been dropped. World War II was over. The United States and its **Allies**, which included Great Britain and the **Soviet Union**, celebrated victory of their defeat of Germany, Japan, and Italy, also known as the **Axis**.

Nations around the world were in ruins. Millions had been killed. Buildings had been destroyed. Many countries were facing economic disaster.

But not the United States. America emerged from the war as the greatest military and economic power in the world. Besides the attack on Pearl Harbor, there had been no battles on American soil. The United States lost 418,500 lives in the deadliest war in history. This was a tragedy. But other countries were in the war much longer. They lost lives in the millions. Germany lost about 6.6 to 8.8 million lives. Poland lost 5.6 million.

World War II, which took the lives of about 3 percent of the world's population, finally ended on September 2, 1945.

Still, Americans felt optimistic about the future. The citizens believed in the ideals of freedom and **democracy**. But they also began worrying about a perceived danger to those ideals.

The threat was coming from the Soviet Union. Despite being an Ally during World War II, the United States had to be wary of the Soviet Union's power and ideologies. The Soviet Union had gone from wartime friend to postwar enemy. It was feared that the nation wanted to spread **communism** around the world. The Cold War had begun.

The Cold War

The seeds of the Cold War were planted during World War II. It began at a February 1945 meeting during the Yalta Conference in the Republic of Crimea. This conference included U.S. President Franklin D. Roosevelt, British Prime Minister Winston Churchill, and Soviet leader Joseph Stalin.

The leaders agreed that the Soviet Union would control Eastern Europe after the war. That included Poland, Hungary, and many other countries. East Germany soon fell under Soviet command. Soon, the Soviets imposed a Communist government and system on the countries it controlled.

Bernard Baruch, a special adviser to several U.S. presidents, was the first to use the term "cold war" to describe the relationship between the United States and the Soviet Union.

At first, only the United States had atomic weapons. However, this changed when the Soviet Union launched its first atomic bomb on August 29, 1949.

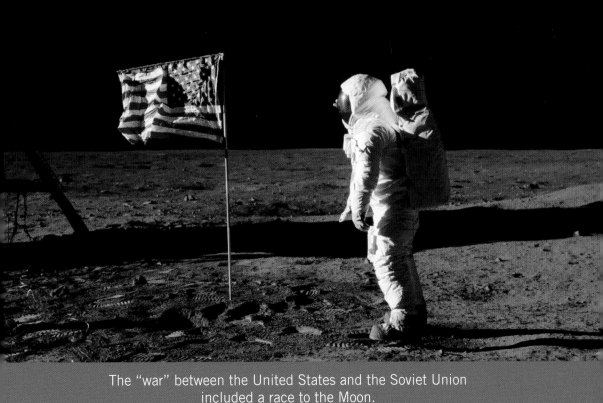

The "war" between the United States and the Soviet Union included a race to the Moon.

Western European nations such as England, France, and West Germany remained democratic. The result was great tension between the two sides. Some Americans worried that the Soviets would try to take Western Europe by force.

The fear grew when the Soviets successfully tested the **atomic** bomb in 1949. They joined the United States in owning the deadliest weapon ever invented. Many Americans feared that the Soviets would use such a bomb on the United States.

The Cold War lasted a long 40 years.

American leaders worked to control the spread of communism abroad and at home. The United States sent troops to help South Korea fight against the invasion of Communist North Korea. Thousands of American soldiers were killed during the Korean War, which was fought between 1950 and 1953. Korea still remains divided today.

The fear of communism and the Soviet Union continued through the 1950s and beyond. It intensified in 1957 when the Russians launched the first **satellite**, *Sputnik 1*, into orbit.

[21ST CENTURY SKILLS LIBRARY]

"The Iron Curtain" was a term that referred to the border that divided the European Communist countries in the east from the non-Communist countries in the west.

Many families and government officials built
fallout shelters across the country.

Americans believed their rival had passed the United States in **technology**. That deepened the fear of war against the Soviet Union. Some Americans even built bomb shelters. They hoped these fallout shelters would allow them to survive a Russian nuclear attack.

This wasn't the only war the United States was facing. There was another war brewing within the United States. It was the war for racial equality.

The Witch Hunts

By 1950, many Americans became **paranoid** that Communist influence had reached their country. That's when Senator Joseph McCarthy of Wisconsin began accusing well-known people of being Communists. These people included members of the movie industry and the military. His investigations ruined many lives. Many people called them "witch hunts," after the people falsely accused of being witches in the late 1600s. McCarthy's witch hunts finally ended in 1954. But they cost many people their jobs and reputations. Think about politics and the world today. Do you see any similarities? Discuss your thoughts with a family member or friend. Ask them what they think.

The Start of the Civil Rights Movement

Two events in the 1950s changed America forever. They would bring the country closer to living out its creed that all people are created equal.

The first was a 1954 decision made by the U.S. Supreme Court. It ruled that **segregated** schools were inherently unequal. The ruling forced school districts across the United States to allow African American students to attend the same public schools as their White peers.

The *Sweatt v. Painter* U.S. Supreme Court case in 1950 helped lay the foundation for the 1954 decision of ruling segregated schools as being unlawful.

That **edict** mostly targeted the South, where laws strictly separated the races. Black schools were greatly inferior to White schools in that part of the country. The thought of Black children attending the same schools as their White children alarmed and angered many parents in the South. It took many years for some schools in the South to **comply** with the Supreme Court order and **integrate** their schools.

Rosa Parks was the secretary of her local chapter of the National Association for the Advancement of Colored People (NAACP), a civil rights organization.

The other historic event that set the civil rights movement in motion occurred on December 1, 1955. That is the day a brave woman named Rosa Parks refused to give up her bus seat to a White man in Montgomery, Alabama. Black people in that city and much of the South had been forced to sit in the back of public buses when White passengers came aboard.

Fifteen-year-old Claudette Colvin was arrested for refusing to give up her seat on a Montgomery bus on March 2, 1955. This happened several months before Rosa Parks was also arrested for the same thing.

The Montgomery bus boycott was the first large-scale political protest against segregation. The boycott lasted from December 5, 1955, to December 20, 1956.

Parks was arrested. But she had set off a firestorm. Black people in Montgomery **boycotted** the buses for more than a year. They walked miles or drove each other in cars to get places. The bus company and local businesses began to lose money.

One man helped lead that boycott. It was a local religious leader named Martin Luther King Jr. He would emerge as the leader of the civil rights movement over the next decade.

The boycott proved to be a great success. African Americans fought for their right to sit wherever they pleased. And they won. The Montgomery bus boycott set off a chain of events resulting in the integration of many public places. These included restaurants, movie theaters, bus terminals, and pools.

The civil rights movement was starting to fight a winning battle. It was working to give Black people a greater opportunity at success in a country with a booming economy and booming population.

The Little Rock Nine

The Supreme Court decision that made school segregation illegal resulted in **resistance** and even violence. Southern governors and local leaders pushed back. Nine Black students showed incredible bravery in the face of White rage in 1957. President Dwight Eisenhower was forced to send in army troops to escort them through angry mobs into Central High School in Little Rock, Arkansas. The Black students remained strong despite harassment and threats all year. They became forever revered as the Little Rock Nine for their courage and strength. What would you have done in their shoes?

The Boom Years

The United States experienced tremendous economic growth after World War II. The country became the richest in the world.

Many U.S. businesses thrived, including the automobile industry. The number of cars America produced from 1946 to 1955 quadrupled. That increase was partly responsible for the new highway systems that linked cities and towns throughout the nation.

The era also featured a housing boom. In 1944, the Servicemen's Readjustment Act, also commonly referred to as the G.I. Bill, helped soldiers adjust back to normal civilian life. Among the G.I. Bill's benefits were favorable housing loans for military families.

During the 1950s, approximately 58 million cars
were purchased by the American people.

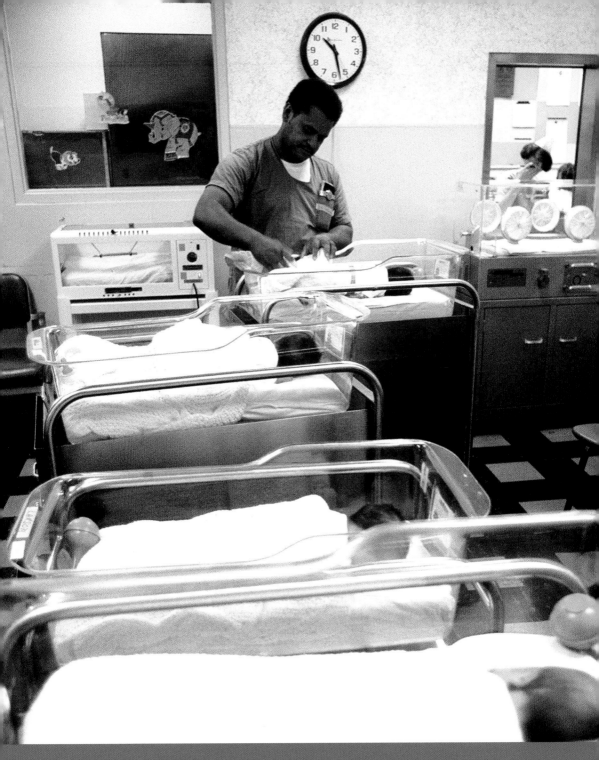

Between 1946 and 1964, approximately 75 billion babies were born!

The G.I. Bill encouraged veterans to own homes and pursue higher education due to low interest rates on loans.

Soldiers returning from the war and their families were encouraged to buy new homes because of this bill. For instance, non-military families had high-**interest** payments and were required to put a certain percentage down when purchasing a home. But for military families, they had low-interest mortgage payments and were not required to give any initial down payment.

During the 1950s, more Americans joined the middle class than ever before.

Many moved away from farms and big northern cities to warm-weather states such as Florida, Arizona, and California. Others made shorter moves from cities to **suburban** areas. Affordable houses were built to accommodate large families near inner cities.

Businesses also moved from cities into the suburbs. Large shopping centers sprang up to meet the needs of the new suburban populations. The number of shopping centers in the United States exploded from 8 at the end of World War II to 3,840 in 1960!

According to historian Lizabeth Cohen, it was deemed
the American duty to contribute to the economy by buying
"more, newer, and better" during the 1950s.

The 1950s and 1960s were considered the "Golden Age of Television." In 1949, less than a million Americans owned a TV set. By 1969, that number rose to 44 million!

When people were not out shopping, many were at home watching a new invention called television. The medium was invented in 1927, but it was not marketed for **consumers** until after the war. In 1946, fewer than 17,000 families across the country owned a television set in their home. Three short years later in 1949, this all changed. By then, Americans were buying sets in droves—as many as 250,000 sets a month!

The average family in 1955 watched about 5 hours of television programs a day. Five years later, three-fourths, or 75 percent, of all American households had at least one television set.

Most Americans felt comfortable with their lives. They were content with how their country was being run. But that was about to change in the 1960s.

The Baby Boom

Soldiers returning home from World War II were ready to start a new life. Many got married and started families. The result was an average of 4.24 million babies born in the United States annually from 1946 to 1964. One motivation for married couples was a strong economy. They felt they could support a large number of children. The economy grew as a result of the baby boom. Products such as toys, sweet cereals, and rock and roll records targeted the new generation of children and teens. What factors have contributed to a smaller number of babies born in America since then?

BRYANT'S GROCERY

Fourteen-year-old Emmett Till came to this site to buy candy in August 1955. White shopkeeper Carolyn Bryant accused the black youth of flirting with her, and shortly thereafter, Till was abducted by Bryant's husband and his half brother. Till's tortured body was later found in the Tallahatchie River. The two men were tried and acquitted but later sold their murder confession to *Look* magazine. Till's death received international attention and is widely credited with sparking the American Civil Rights Movement.

PLACED DURING THE 50TH ANNIVERSARY OF THE FREEDOM RIDES · 1961-2011

Emmett Till's murder further sparked the civil rights movement as his brutal death shocked America and the world.

Research & Act

Perhaps the most horrifying event in 1950s America was the murder of 14-year-old Emmett Till. While visiting his cousin and uncle in Mississippi in August of 1954, two men brutally took his life. Till was tortured and tossed into a river. An all-White jury later ruled the murderers to be innocent. The two accused men later admitted to the crime in a magazine article but remained free. Till's mother ordered that her son's beaten face be shown for everyone to see at his funeral. Research the reasons for her decision. Then, write your opinion on that decision.

Timeline

▶ February 4–11, 1945: **The Yalta Conference determines that the Soviet Union will control the countries of Eastern Europe after World War II.**

▶ August 29, 1949: **The Cold War intensifies as the Soviet Union completes its first atomic bomb test.**

▶ February 9, 1950: **Senator Joseph McCarthy makes the first charges of Communist influence in the United States during a speech in West Virginia.**

▶ June 25, 1950: **The Korean War begins.**

▶ July 27, 1953: **The Korean War ends with an armistice.**

▶ April 22, 1954: **The U.S. Senate censures Joseph McCarthy. The persecution of those accused of communism ends.**

▶ May 17, 1954: **The Supreme Court rules in *Brown v. Board of Education of Topeka* that segregated schools goes against the U.S. Constitution.**

▶ December 1, 1955: **Rosa Parks refuses to give up her bus seat to a White man in Montgomery, Alabama. The Montgomery bus boycott begins.**

▶ September 24, 1957: **President Eisenhower sends army troops to Little Rock, Arkansas, to ensure the admission of nine Black students to Central High School.**

▶ January 1, 1959: **Communist leader Fidel Castro takes over Cuba, elevating Cold War fears in the United States.**

Further Research

BOOKS

Colbert, Brandy, and Jeanne Theoharis. *The Rebellious Life of Mrs. Rosa Parks.* Boston, MA: Beacon Press, 2020.

Gitlin, Martin. *The Montgomery Bus Boycott: A History Perspectives Book.* Ann Arbor, MI: Cherry Lake Publishing, 2014.

Goodman, Keith. *The Cold War Explained for Kids.* Independently published, 2017.

WEBSITES

Ducksters—World War II: After the War
https://www.ducksters.com/history/world_war_ii/after_ww2.php

National Geographic Kids—Hero for All: Martin Luther King Jr.
https://kids.nationalgeographic.com/explore/history/martin-luther-king-jr

Glossary

Allies (AL-eyze) countries fighting alongside the United States in World War II

atomic (uh-TAH-mik) powered by nuclear energy

Axis (AXZ-is) countries fighting against the United States in World War II

boycotted (BOY-kott-uhd) refused to buy or use something on moral grounds

communism (KAHM-yuh-nih-zuhm) a system of government with single-party control of production

comply (kuhm-PLY) to do what another person or group requests

consumers (kuhn-SOO-muhrz) people who buy and use products and services

democracy (dih-MAH-kruh-see) a government in which the supreme power is held by the people

edict (EE-dikt) an official order or command

integrate (IN-tuh-grayt) to allow people of different races to go to the same public places

interest (IN-trist) the money paid by a borrower for the use of borrowed money

paranoid (PAIR-uh-noyd) to be afraid of something for no legitimate reason

resistance (rih-ZIH-stuhnss) to fight back against laws or policies believed to be unfair

satellite (SAH-tuh-lyte) human-made object intended to orbit Earth or the moon

segregated (SEH-grih-gay-tuhd) a place or business in which only selected groups of people are allowed to be

Soviet Union (SOH-vee-uht YOON-yuhn) a federation made up of Russia and several other smaller countries

suburban (suh-BUHR-buhn) smaller community close to or surrounding an urban center

technology (tek-NAH-luh-jee) the use of science in solving problems or creating new things

INDEX